SPEECH

OF THE

HON. THOMAS EWING,

AT

CHILLICOTHE, OHIO,

BEFORE A REPUBLICAN MASS MEETING, SEPTEMBER 29th, 1860.

CINCINNATI:
RICKEY, MALLORY & CO., 75 WEST FOURTH STREET.

1860.

SPEECH:

My Friends and Fellow Citizens:

I am here to address you by the invitation of your Republican Central Committee. I belong to no existing party. I am attached to none, but to the Union—the States—their liberties and laws. I come not to arouse your enthusiasm in behalf of any man or any party, but to speak my own free thoughts, and the conclusions of my own judgment, as to the condition of our country and the course—of all that are open to us—which is most likely to tend to its permanent prosperity and peace. I will speak something of men, but more of principle and policy.

And it may be proper for me to say, in the outset, that I have made up my mind to vote for Abraham Lincoln. I know him personally, and am satisfied with him. He is a man of unimpeached integrity—sufficiently acquainted with the recent history of our country, and the men and measures which have made up that history. I am satisfied with the man, though I do not place him in advance of all his opponents. John Bell is his equal in personal qualities, of large experience, the elder statesman, and if we could make him our President, I would consider him a very safe choice. I know him much more intimately than Mr. Lincoln. I was in counsel with him daily for many months in times of trial, and besides my confidence in the statesman, I have for him a warm feeling of personal friendship and regard.

But he can not get the vote of Ohio. His ticket is but a disturbing element in the canvass. The contest in this State is between Lincoln and Douglas, and between them I can not hesitate for a moment, and indeed, have no vote to throw away when such is the contest.

As a statesman, Douglas has shown himself inconsiderate and reckless. The extreme agitation of the country for the past six years is due to his restless impatience for notoriety. He is politically answerable for all the terrible atrocities consequent upon the repeal of the Missouri Compromise. They were embodied in the repeal, and the eye of a statesman could not have failed to discern them there. He set a complicated machine, which he understood not, in wild and destructive motion, and his sole merit, is that he attempted but knew not how to check or direct its movement. Experience of the past does not warrant us in believing that the Republic would be safe under his guidance. It would be once again Phæton guiding the chariot of the sun.

Mr. Breckinridge I know only as a gentleman, and as such I esteem him and believe him stainless. He has no record as a statesman, at least none known to me; and he stands as the representative of an extreme sectional party, whose opinions and policy tend strongly to disunion. Besides, Lane, the candidate for Vice President, is, I think, little worthy of that honorable position. My opinion of his personal merits will be found at large in a speech delivered in the Senate of the United States, January 7, 1851, on the Bradbury resolutions, which, with accompanying documents, is in Appendix to Congressional Globe, vol. 23, pages 67 and 68.

This will suffice for the personal merits and status of the several candidates. The political questions involved, and my own relation to those questions, require a more careful presentation.

I view the existing contest almost from a neutral stand point. I have belonged to no political party since the 22d day of March, 1854, but have since that time looked upon the acts and purposes of each as subjects of approval or censure, solely and only as in my opinion their efforts might be useful or injurious to the country.

The Republican party arose out of the repeal of the Missouri Compromise. This attempt, when first made, seemed an act of wanton childish recklessness, and took the nation by surprise. The people in no section of the Union desired it, or thought of it. That Compromise was the settlement of a difficult and dangerous question, with which thinking men of all sections were satisfied. The proposed repeal was received in the South with no approbation. I myself heard Southern Senators speak of it as meddlesome and officious—a thing which annoyed them greatly. Their ablest statesmen disapproved of it and would have resisted it had they not feared that demagogues at home might use it to their injury. In the North it excited indignation and alarm. While the measure was still pending in Congress—and it was a long time pending—a convention was called to meet at Columbus, the avowed object of which was to combine the elements of opposition to that, irrespective of all other political issues. This was the seed-germ of the Republican party.

It was a movement for the success of which I felt deep solicitude. I had no fears of the permanent establishment of slavery in Kansas or Nebraska, but I foresaw the disorders to which the repeal must give rise, and I greatly feared that the movement itself, under the guidance of extreme party leaders acting upon aroused public feeling, might be pushed beyond its legitimate object, and by attempting too much, fail in that, and do evil and not good by the effort. I wished to move the rock and leave the mountain at rest but I feared that our engineers would attempt both and fail in both. The object of the organization is shown by a letter of the State Central Committee, asking me to attend and address the Convention; and my fears that it would fail by attempting too much, or turning aside from its avowed purpose, are shown in an extract from my reply, which I take the liberty to read:

LETTER OF INVITATION.

COLUMBUS, Ohio, March 2d, 1854.

Hon. Thos. Ewing, Lancaster, Ohio.

You will see by the newspapers of this city, that a Mass Convention of the people of Ohio, without distinction of party, has been called to meet in this city, on the 22d day of March next. It is proposed that the Convention consist of all who are opposed to the repeal of the Missouri Compromise, and the introduction of slavery into Kansas and Nebraska.

The undersigned Committee of Correspondence earnestly invite you to attend the Convention as one of the speakers on the occasion, Signed,

E. R. ECKLEY.

In my reply, after a brief discussion of the ordinances and laws which make up the history of the division of our unoccupied territory between free and slave labor, I say:

EXTRACT FROM ANSWER.

"The free and slave territory must be separated by a law, prior to its occupation or it will at no distant day separate itself in a manner greatly more injurious to the peace and good order of society. We can not ask our free laborers to mingle and associate with slaves without forgetting the dignity and importance of labor as a social and political element in our Northern communities.

"The Missouri Compromise makes this separation. It was a wise and well considered measure. Its repeal would be a great wrong and a great evil. As such, we ought to resist and if possible, avert it. On this the people of the North, almost as a body and a goodly portion of the South will unite. Let us engage in it in a manner becoming the subject—with calmness, prudence and consideration—and by no means suffer ourselves to be defeated in this, which we all feel to be just, right and necessary, by blending with it, or suffering to be involved with it, any other object, however desirable to many. Let us take this single and alone. In any departure from the plain straightforward path to the one sole object there is danger—danger of division, and with division defeat. We can probably prevent the infliction of the anticipated wrong; if not we can certainly in due time and by constitutional means redress it.

"I have purposely confined myself to the political and practical view of this subject, as in my opinion, it embraces the true principle of the measure which it is the object of the Convention to sustain.

"Be kind enough to make known my concurrence in the expressed objects of the Convention, and my conviction that if pursued calmly and wisely, they can not fail of ultimate success." I am, very respectfully yours,

T. EWING.

Messrs. E. R. Eckley and others.

In signifying my approbation of the objects of the Convention, I was careful to use the qualifying term "expressed," as I had little doubt that many who engaged in the movement would attempt, and I feared successfully, to extend it to other and widely different purposes. My apprehensions were realized. The Convention was composed of a large proportion of extreme anti-slavery men, it was led by extreme men, and it passed resolutions which in effect abandoned opposition to the repeal of the Missouri Compromise—resolutions which, indeed, could not be carried out without the repeal, virtual, if not actual. In short, those who composed the Convention determined to reject the division of territory made by the Missouri Compromise, and go into a fight at large—a kind of irrepressible conflict against the holders of slaves in general—while the admission of Kansas as a Free State was but an inconsiderable incident in the progress of their proposed action. Indeed, it must necessarily have arrested that progress and defeated the ultimate object of the leaders of that body. Their speeches announced and resolutions prescribed a course of political action which involved as one of its essential elements, not the restoration but the permanent abandonment of the Missouri Compromise.

The expressed object of the original organization—the restoration of that compromise, had met my approbation; I united, therefore, in its pursuit with men of widely different opinions on kindred subjects; but because I united with them in *this*, I could, therefore, not allow them to prescribe for me new laws of thought and action. They turned to the pursuit of other objects which must, as I believed, produce mighty mischiefs in their process of development—a policy which involved a long and fierce conflict, and which left the question of Freedom or Slavery in the Territories, covered by the Missouri Compromise, unsettled while the war was waged; and it left Kansas, especially, delivered over to anarchy and violence. This necessarily cut off from the party many thousands who had in purpose or in act united in the original object, and who still continued to desire and promote that object. It drew a strictly sectional party line, which no one could pass, and necessarily involved the selection of a party leader who would be nothing more or less or other than the representative embodiment of the sectional party, and it as necessarily excluded any man of national opinion or reputation. Parties of many discordant opinions were to be united in the canvass; it was, therefore, essential that their leader should have no record. Hence, in 1856, Mr. Fremont, a gentleman quite unknown in the political or public history of our country, was selected as their candidate for President, and the *party* was defeated, while the *original principle* triumphed. For as far as public opinion had potency, Kansas was virtually a Free State on the day Mr. Buchanan took his seat as President.

Thus, the original issue on which the Republican organization was put to the country, was tried and sustained, while the *party* which had abandoned it was defeated. And if Mr. Buchanan had regarded the clear indications of public will, and had facilitated the admission of Kansas under a constitution of her own adoption, the Republican party must have placed itself on national ground and sustained itself on general principles of national policy, or ceased at once to be a power in the land. But he and his advisers seemed to be struck with judicial blindness. Against all right, and truth, and justice, and against the obvious sense of a large majority of the nation, they attempted to force a forged and false Constitution on Kansas, which was to make it a Slave State in contempt of the opinions of nine-tenths of its inhabitants. They persevered in the wrong even after they were fairly whipped out of it. And when thus beaten beyond all possibility of recuperation, they kept the question open by refusing to admit Ksnsas as a Free State under a Constitution of her own adoption. Those who organized themselves under the name of the Republican party, to exclude Slavery from Kansas and Nebraska, virtually accomplished their object—it had become morally impossible for Slavery to be forced into Kansas; but Mr. Buchanan kept the question open, and thus kept the Republican party united, vigorous and active by intriguing to prevent full and immediate consummation of its victory. That party, though the ultimate accomplishment of the object of its organization was rendered certain, had not yet actually accomplished it; and it must live till it fulfilled its destiny. But, as I have said, men of differing and discordant opinions in other matters, united in this: Abolitionists, higher law and irrepressible conflict men—all shades and degrees—up to and including the solid phalanx of Whig principles and opinion. And it happened in this case, as in most others, that extreme men were the busy, active men always on the alert, little regarding the one purpose which united the great mass of the people, except in so far as it could be used as an instrument for their ulterior objects. They called and took control of conventions, and through them of many of the States. And the people acted with them, for they were ostensibly pursuing the great object all had in view; while the folly of the Administration excused them in public opinion when they departed from or tresspassed beyond that object. By this means the people of some of the States North and West were placed in a false position—misrepresented as to their opinions and feelings by the public acts of their constituted authorities. In Ohio, extreme men ruled and seemed to be the majority, but they never were so. As in an effervescing fluid, all seems foam to those who look only on its surface, so did this element seem to be all of the party opposed to the repeal of the Missouri Compromise, while in truth its strength lay in the calm, conservative Whig mass, which remained inactive below. As examples in our own State, of extreme party action, witness the attack last year upon the independence of the Judiciary in the person of Judge Swan—the refusal of the Legislature last winter, when the subject was before them, to pass a law to prohibit the forming or fitting out in Ohio the marauding expeditions against our sister States. The bill in form and substance being as nearly as possible identical with a law of the United States, as to nations with whom we are at peace; and, which indeed, modern civilization has introduced into the codes of nearly all nations not piratical; and the refusal of our Executive to surrender fugitives from justice—pursuant to the requirements of the Constitution* all which indicated that this party was

* This, I find, is a heresy of some ten years standing, a fact which had escaped me, as I was too busily engaged in organizing a new department at Washington, at the time it arose, to give much attention to passing events. Our present Governor, however, is not responsible for it, but it is not the less a heresy, and highly injurious, especially in the connection in which I have placed it. It is said, in the opinion of the Attorney General of that day, that this provision of the Constitution ought not to be extended, 1st. To cases not within the rule observed by the comity of nations; or 2nd. The cases designated in our treaties with foreign nations; 3d. Or crimes known to the common law; 4th. Or such as are recognized as crimes in the State called on to surrender the fugitive. Now, neither

engaged in a conflict which must be, in fact and deed *irrepressible* so long as it and the Union both endured; and that the organic law of the republic had been superseded by a *higher* or *lower* law—namely, the individual will, dominant in the minds of excited men. Such was the condition of things which caused me to stand aloof from the party, the objects of whose original organization I approved, and to advance which objects I labored afterwards *out of the party* earnestly, and, I have reason to believe, effectively.

But I looked for a reaction, and it has come. Conservative men, law-loving and law-abiding men, could not suffer the excesses of the time to go abroad under their apparent sanction and remain inactive. The reaction pre-

---

one or all of these criteria will serve as a test, for 1st. There is no comity of nations as to extradition of criminals, as such. 2nd. Our treaties designate the special crimes, and among them are not to be found the highest, namely *treason*, nor one half of the high crimes known to the laws of every civilized state and country, as *burglary*, *larceny*, *rape*, *bigamy*, *incest*, *perjury*, etc., etc., etc. 3rd. The common law omits, of course, all crimes having their origin in the present changed condition of society, such as the malicious destruction of canal locks, reservoirs, etc., and the maliciously placing obstructions on railroads with intent to destroy life; and the fourth test, namely, that it must be a crime by the law of the State called on to make the surrender, would be subject to the last named difficulty, for Florida, Arkansas and Oregon could not surrender a fugitive who should be charged capitally with a crime against the canals, or railroads of other States. But the conclusive objection is, that the constitution gives no possible pretext for any such limited construction. The crime must be committed in the State making the demand, by a person actually within it; the laws of that State, therefore, must govern it; and as to the degree of the crime, the enumeration by the Constitution is in the descending series,—"Treason, felony, or *other* crime." That is, *lesser* crime.

As to what is said of trivial offenses, it seems to me clear that it is for the State whose laws declare the crime, to judge. The Constitution might well presume that no State would make an act criminal out of mere wantonness or folly. Nor can it be supposed that an offender would flee, or the executive of a State demand a fugitive except in cases where the offense was great, or greatly injurious to society.

sented itself in a two-fold aspect. Out of the party, by the Union organization in the North—in the party, by the rejection of extreme party leaders and the nomination of a sound conservative man for President at the late Chicago Convention.

The resolutions of the Chicago Convention—the platform—is better than we have been accustomed to, in speeches and resolves, for four or five years past—better in its positions, much better in tone and temper. It quite rejects the heresy that any law applicable to the civil government of our Union is *higher* than the Constitution of the United States. It condemns in strong terms the organization of marauding expeditions in any of the States to attack the people or the institutions of neighboring States, (a thing which the Ohio Legislature had so recently refused to declare unlawful;) and in its whole tone and temper counsels, peace and mutual respect of each other's rights between States, instead of the maintenance of a continual and irrepressible conflict. It also has discovered and declares that the nation has a mission other than that of perpetual war over Slavery. And especially it advances *sound* old Whig doctrine as to the fostering care which Government owes to the industry of its people. This suits me well. It is a recurrence to first principles—a strong assurance that the party, as it now exists, intends to build up and preserve, and not pull down and destroy.

But I do not think the adoption of a portion of the Declaration of Independence in very good taste, and such indeed seemed to be the opinion of a majority of the Convention; but beyond that it is quite unimportant. The clause adopted is true in the vague and general sense in which it was used by the framers of the Declaration, who were three-fourths of them slaveholders. And in that sense it seems to have been taken by the Convention; for if not, it would be inconsistent with their other resolves, which assert in express terms the absolute right of States slave and free, over their domestic institutions.

I object to the eighth resolution. The proposition "that the normal condition of all the territory of the United States is that of freedom," is not true in point of fact. The *rule*, the *norma*, which is announced by the proposition, must apply if it has any meaning, to the territory as it stood at the time of the formation of the Constitution, when slavery existed under and by the law of nearly all the States and in all the Territories, except the territory northwest of the river Ohio; and as to the after acquired territory, the *norma* or *rule* must be applied to its condition at the moment it became the property of the United States. And Louisiana, all that is now in question, was *then* slave territory.

The framers of the Constitution had no conception of this "*normal condition.*" When they willed that the North-Western territory should be free, it was so declared by the adoption of the ordinance of 1787, with its prohibitory clause as binding under the Constitution. The South-Western Territory was left to slavery just where the laws of North Carolina and Georgia had held it. The ships sailing under the flag and carrying papers under the seal of the United States, attesting their nationality, are wherever they may sail on the high seas, part and parcel of the territory of the United States, and under the dominion, pure and unmixed, of her Constitution and laws: and who would be bold enough to contend that prior to the year 1808, while the Constitution forbade the abolition of the slave trade, that the "normal condition" of the ships which bore the slaves was "that of freedom?" Surely they had no condition *whatever* except that which the Constitution, and the laws passed under it, created. I feel it clear to a demonstration that the proposition as to the "normal condition" of the territories of the United States in its most general or more restricted sense can not be maintained.

The other branch of the resolution, namely the proposition, that Congress has but a limited power over slavery in the Territories, though advanced by the Chicago Convention in this eighth resolution,—by the Breckinridge Convention in their second resolution, and sustained by the Supreme Court of the United States, in the case of Dred Scott *vs.* Sandford, does not command the assent of my judgment. But if the proposition that the power of Congress over the Territories is *limited* in that particular be true, the Breckinridge Convention and the Supreme Court of the United States have the best of argument, to say nothing of authority. But, with all my habitual deference and respect for that Court, and I think it second to none in the world for the qualities which give weight and dignity to a judicial tribunal, I can not divest myself of the opinion that it erred on this point, which was quite unnecessary to the decision of the case.

Their error, in my judgment, consists in considering slaves as property merely; instead of considering master and slave as relations, which in our artificial system, man holds to man. The latter is the view taken of it in the Constitution of the United States. Slaves in that instrument are not treated as property, any more than minor children, apprentices, or men bound by contract to perform labor. Under the Constitution, property is not represented—persons owing service are. If property escape from one State and go into another, the Constitution does not direct that it shall be delivered up. If persons owing service escape, it does so direct. Congress is empowered to regulate commerce between the States. Commerce has to do with property. But the States exercise the sole power of admitting or prohibiting the importation from other States of persons owing service—in this their laws treat them not as property. Congress has the express power to regulate foreign commerce, but is denied the power until the year 1808 to prohibit the imigration or importation into any of the States now existing, of such persons as the said State shall think proper to admit. This implies the power to prohibit their importation into any new State or into any Territory, and the argument also involves this dilemma: If slaves are *property* merely, under the Constitution, Congress can prohibit their importation into any Territory by virtue of its power to regulate commerce between the States. If they be not *property*, but *persons*, the power of the sovereign (which the Supreme Court says Congress is) to regulate and fix the relations of man to man in the Territory is without any limitation, expressed or implied. Congress has, in this point of view, the same power to prohibit slavery, so far as property exists in the labor of the slave, as it would have to make the son free at twenty, instead of twenty-one, thus depriving the father of one year of his labor. And I have so much confidence in the high character and elevated feeling and sense of justice of the Court, that I do not doubt the question will be re-considered when a new case arises, if it ever do arise, which shall require its application.

But, if we admit, with the eighth resolution of the Chicago Convention, that the power of Congress is limited in the Territories over that one special subject matter—I know not where to find an argument potent enough to resist the conclusion of the Supreme Court, sustained as it is by its high judicial authority.

No vague generalities will avail anything on either side. No general purpose of gradual emancipation strong enough to affect the question can be found written down in the Constitution—none to satisfy the legal mind that it was intended to deny Congress the power to admit slavery in the territories, when such generality, if any bear that aspect, is found side by side with the clause forbidding Congress to prohibit the slave trade for twenty years. The Declaration of Independence is cited, but it contains nothing, which upon sound legal construction could sustain the position even if all its language were inserted in the Constitution. But this Declaration was written about fourteen years before the Constitution, and the common construction requires us to admit, that all in the former instrument, not consistent with the latter was reconsidered and rejected. Nor do I think it safe to infer from other generalities equally vague, touching the rights of property, which, in the language of the Constitution, slaves are not, that Congress is denied the power to exclude slavery from the territories, when such generality is found side by side with an implication quite as potent as a direct enactment, which authorizes Congress at once to prohibit the importation of slaves anywhere except into States exising at the time of the formation of the Constitution. I would that the eighth resolution of the Chicago Convention were not in its platform. It seems to be there for no other purpose than to give opponents advantage in the argument. It is an abstraction, unless in every practical sense, as it is false in fact and logic.

I know of but one case in which the *normal* question can arise, namely: in a registered American ship at sea. She sails or steams from Baltimore to New Orleans. Is a slave on board this ship free as soon as he is beyond the jurisdiction of any of the States? And if he be, may Congress change this rule by law? Here is the *normal* condition, with its attendant consequences, and here is the only place in which I can conceive that the irrepressible conflict can be kept up. It must be fought out on shipboard—it can not live on land. Still I can consent to let this abstract fallacy pass—reject the resolution and support the nomination, for I have no doubt that Mr. Lincoln, himself a sound lawyer, will esteem the Constitution of the United States superior to this section of the platform. It is impossible, without assumption, which can be made on one side as well as the other, to rest the admission or rejection of slavery in our present Territories on any other ground than that of its status when it became part of the United States, or the subsequent Acts of Congress, or territorial law affecting it. Forced assumptions and bold assertions will not avail—they convince nobody that reasons—and the Constitution, which speaks intelligible language, and the law of nations leave the question where I have found it. The status or normal condition of Louisiana was that of a slave territory. The Missouri Compromise gave all of it north of 36 degrees 30 minutes to Freedom. The repeal of that compromise left it subject to the laws of the territories until they are negatived by Congress. Hence the importance of the original formation of the Republican party, and its maintenance on its original ground, and for its original objects, until those objects shall be accomplished —until it shall have fulfilled its destiny. Admitting that the institution of slavery is equal for the welfare of a State with that of freedom, which I do not think it is, (others do, and I have no right to force my opinion on them,) admitting this, we all know that the free and slave labor will not mingle. The free white man will not work with the negro slave in the same shop, or in the same field, because in his opinion it degrades him. Labor ceases to be honorable when it is especially the vocation of slaves. Hence emigration goes only from a free State, to a free state or territory. The new slave States and Territories are, therefore, shut out from immigration of free laborers as fully as the free State and Territories from the slave. The lines are passed by a few, but such is the general fact.

Louisiana was the general property of the Union. Its normal condition was that of slave territory, but it was not right that it should all remain so. The different sections of the Union could not use and enjoy it together—it was therefore, just, and wise, and proper, that it should be divided between them so that each should enjoy his part to the best advantage; and the repeal of the Missouri Compromise broke up this just and well considered partition, which it is the mission of the Republican party actually or virtually to restore. The slave States have their share of the Territory—it is most ample for their wants. The free States must also have theirs. They must have it, not because they are the stronger, and can hold it—not because their institutions are better than those of the South, and therefore the one and not the other ought to be extended—for to claim this in attempting a peaceful adjustment, were arrogance which would offend—not argument that would convince. But we are entitled to it by original right as our just partition—we are entitled to it by compromise and mutual agreement. And our rights asserted firmly, with dignified courtesy, will be much more readily conceded than if we mingled with their assertion, contumely and reproach. This disposed of—and I think we shall dispose of it amicably—the irrepressible conflict will be repressed, for there will be nothing remaining for which a conflict can be maintained.

Having fulfilled this its mission, the Republican party can not possibly maintain itself as a general Anti-Slavery party. The whole North was aroused to resist or redress a wrong. Old Whigs, old Democrats—men almost without respect to previous party distinctions, united in this, and their united effort and full success was only prevented by the fears of some that they meditated an opposite wrong while redressing this. But when the end is attained, and the cause ceases, the organization must cease with it, or it must be placed on some other and more permanent basis.

But as I have said, it can not have success as a general anti-slavery party. The anti-slavery feeling in the North is strong enough and universal—no man wants slavery with us or near us—but it is a feeling of resistance—not of attack. We must be satisfied that there is an attempt meditated to obtrude slavery upon our free Territories in order to call that feeling into action, and make it control the opinion and conduct of the mass of our people. That the actual conflict is ended, I have no doubt. Indeed the attempt to extend slavery into Kansas, even if it had been possible to effect it, was as unwise as it was unjust. Slavery as an existing thing, can not be taken into new Territories, without losing its hold on border States,—and its extension into Kansas must have greatly hastened emancipation in Missouri, which is only a question of time. It was recently said by Stevens, of Georgia, in a speech delivered in Augusta, that Slavery can not be extended judiciously, to new Territories, without re-opening the Slave Trade, to which he declared himself opposed. The same opinion was also expressed, though I do not now recollect the occasion, by Mr. Hammond, of South Carolina. That impression is becoming general in the South—it was therefore not their wise men who devised the extension of Slavery into Kansas. I have hence a right to conclude that the conflict is ended, so far as it depends upon Southern aggression. I conclude also, that the Republican party will within the present or early part of the coming year have fulfilled its original destiny, and must end also, or place itself on a basis of substantial national policy. An effort to this effect is made in the platform of the Chicago Convention, and generally I like the direction to which it points. It contains, however, one element useful perhaps for the present year, but fatal if made to hold its place in the future—an incorporation of the general anti-slavery element in connection with its many sound principles of national policy. This will do while the attempt to force slavery upon a territory free by contract is continued; but when that is past, settled, signed and sealed, it will then make it sectional. The leaders of the party claim for it a dominion of twenty years; something more than one political generation. They are mistaken if they fasten to it this sectional fallacy—an abstraction, false, useless, pregnant with evil—an apple of discord and disunion. It cuts off all possible support from the Southern States and all the conservative support in the North and West. Erase it—wipe it out, and the party may live its twenty years; retain it and it will but just survive the election of its President.

I have little doubt of the election of Mr. Lincoln. He is an old Whig. He has had his political training in a highly conservative party, of which he was a calm, considerate and reasoning member. And though he has passed through a fierce conflict—in which the aggression of slavery was the subject of attack and defense—which would naturally tend to deflect both expression and opinion, and in which he has probably said some things not strictly canonical, I doubt not that the feeling which that conflict excited has passed away, and that from the first to the last—in his inaugural address in which words will be things, and in his final message he will show himself the President of the nation, not of a section or a party. Then if misfortune come upon the country, he and all of us may feel that no uncalled for word or inconsiderate act of his will have caused it. Fortunately, he will not be thrown upon an extreme party for support. The conservative interest nominated, and that also will elect him.

Mr. Bell, if I mistake not, will have but small support in the Northwestern States—not because he is less worthy than Mr. Lincoln, but because he enters the canvass with no prospect of success before the people; and it is the part of wisdom to attempt the good that is practicable—not that which is impossible. Indeed, it were wise for the especial friends of Mr. Bell to support Mr. Lincoln here; and show him that the conservative interest on which he may rely is strong. But especially a contest against him is unwise on their part. If the election go to the House, the chance of Mr. Bell for success there were greatly improved, by the fact that he has friends and well wishers among the supporters of Mr. Lincoln.

Such, fellow citizens, are some of the views which I entertain of the condition of our country, and the coming political contest. Much has been said and done on both sides of the line to educate our people for disunion—to cultivate that mutual hatred and distrust which sets nations to war against each other, dissolves States and breaks up families. Of this we have everywhere too much, but it is becoming less and less to the public taste. Still I can not hope it will cease, for it is an inconceivably easy mode of being virtuous ourselves to forget our own faults, and attack and abhor the imputed vices of our neighbors. There are, indeed, many on both sides of the line who cry aloud for disunion; but they are in all cases, as far as I know, a safe distance from the line of contest. They are brave men who can, with unshaken nerves *look upon*, or rather *read of*, the strife and bloodshed and ruin and misery which such a conflict, if they can excite it, must bring upon the more exposed portions of our people. Some talk of a peaceful dissolution of the Union; but with a people such as ours, perhaps with any people, that is impossible. The late terrible scenes in Kansas prove it. We are of a noble race, possessed in a high degree of vigor and energy and courage; but once freed from the restraints of law and social order, as fierce and cruel as lions' whelps that have tasted blood. And if disunion should come, it would not be peaceful, but bloody, and all that is fierce and cruel in the land would meet in mutual vengeance and rapine on the line of conflict.

But in my opinion the late imminent danger to

the Republic is passed. I feel that the subject of controversy, all that is worthy of a statesman's regard has passed and is about to pass away. Still, angry feelings will exist; popular declaimers can not spare a subject on which it is so easy to be eloquent and on which all can be eloquent alike; but that mutual distrust and hatred which, more than all else, endangers the union, will gradually subside, if the PEOPLE elect their President, and if wisdom and prudence control his official actions.

www.ingramcontent.com/pod-product-compliance
Lightning Source LLC
LaVergne TN
LVHW011145110826
845150LV00008B/2512

* 9 7 8 1 4 1 8 1 9 1 9 2 4 *